www.InnovativeThunder.com

THIS BOOK IS FOR EVERYONE WHO WANTS TO MOVE INTO THE DIGITAL ERA OF AWESOMENESS.

YEAH.

"You watch TV, you read magazines, but you hang out online. In Digital Media the consumer becomes a user. ...

OH MY GOD WHAT HAPPENED?

... And that is where advertising ends to be just advertising. Now the solution can be a real advantage to the people. ...

GOOD TO KNOW ABOUT TECHNOLOGY:

GOOD TO KNOW FOR YOUR IDEAS:

... And trough this, it is much easier to create a relationship between a brand and the people."

OH MY GOD WHAT HAPPENED?

A lot of things have happened during the past few years. Digital media have become far more than just toys for nerds – they now have an impact on every-body's life to a greater extent than ever before. From the cell phone in your pocket and industries fighting to survive down to your old high-school friend you block on Facebook to prevent him from bothering you every time you're online.

We're currently experiencing a time of change, a change in that a whole generation is evolving; this generation is growing up with an entirely new media behavior. It's a generation that can't imagine a world that is not digital.

Under this paradigm, the marketing industry must adapt, since you can hardly reach this generation using means and methods from the past. What's the right way to deal with these changes? What do you have to be aware of and what do marketing guys need to do to stay at it?

Before we dive deep into the world of digital awesome-ness, let's take a look back one more time:

What has actually happened?

1969 - 1983

1969: The Internet is born.
In order to link universities with research facilities, the Advanced Research Project Agency run by the US Department of Defense developed ARPANET, which served as the basis of the Internet as we know it today. Rumor has it that the original objective of this project, against the backdrop of the Cold War, was to develop a distributed communication system to ensure fail-safe communication in case of a nuclear war.

1971: The first e-mail.
Ray Tomlinson, inventor of e-mail, sends a message to his colleagues in 1971 and informs them about the fact that from then on, it was possible to send news via a network by adding the @-icon and the computer's host name to the addressee's user name. In Germany, the first e-mail is received on August 3rd, 1984, at 10:14 CET. Under his address, "rotert@germany", Michael Rotert at Karlsruhe University receives greetings, which were sent the day before.

1983: The cell phone.
Motorola releases the first commercial cell phone. It costs nearly $4,000 and allows talking for only one hour.

1989 - 1990

1989: The WorldWideWeb is born.

In order to keep the data chaos at the CERN research center within a limit, Tim Berners-Lee, a Brit who works there as a computer scientist, lays down his "Information management" white paper. Many consider this to be the birth certificate of the World Wide Web. The idea of the first browser to move within the World Wide Web is also Tim's idea. Its name, "World Wide Web", became a synonym for the Internet as a whole.

1989: The invention of the MP3.

Karlheinz Brandenburger completes his doctoral thesis, "Digital Music Compression", which he had begun in 1982 at the Frauenhofer-Institut as well as at the Friedrich-Alexander University in Erlangen-Nuremberg. The research he and his team embarked on facilitated the birth of the music industry's nightmare: the MP3.

1988/90: DSL pushes the Internet.

DSL makes it suddenly possible to receive data ten times as fast as with a regular 56k modem. Finally, this new high-speed Internet allows listening to music and watching movies in real-time.

1990: Accessing the Internet with your cell phone.

From the beginning of the nineties, it is possible for the consumer to access the Internet via the GSM net, even though this access is at low speed.

1993 - 1994

1993: The golden Shield.

China launches its blocking program for anti-regime content on the Internet. They call it "The Golden Shield" or "The Great Firewall of China".

1993: The first CD burners hit the market.

In combination with the invention of the MP3, a lethal duo evolves, since it is now possible for anybody to burn his or her own music and to trade or even sell it.

1994/95: The foundation of Yahoo.

David Filo and Jerry Yang work on a navigation aid for the Internet. The number of Internet sites registered in the web catalogue, a kind of telephone directory for the Internet, was growing simply too rapidly. So, they started categorizing them. This turned out to be the cornerstone for one of the most successful brands of the Internet. Its name: Yahoo.

1994: The first banner ads are sold.

HotWired is the first company to sell banner ads on a large scale. The first buyers: AT&T and Zima. The click rate, the number of clicks on one banner in relation to its overall number of views, is 30%! Today, it is already considered a success when the 1% barrier is reached.

1997 - 1998

1997: Blank CDs enter the charts.

In 1997, music, downloaded illegally from the Internet, burnt on CD and sold illegally, is the trigger for the worldwide crisis of the sound carrier industry. For the first time, in 2001, more blank CDs (182m) are sold than recorded CDs (172m).

1998: College Kid destroys the music industry.

Shawn Fanning programmes the peer-to-per music-sharing tool "Napster" and thus plunges the already very weakened music industry into an unrivalled crisis it is still recovering from today.

1998: Google.

Google.com goes online as a test version and is one of the first "real" search engines where a program combs through the Net, not an editorial department. In the year of its foundation, Google already knows 25 million sites and has become the worldwide leader on the search engine market with 80% of all search requests.

1998: The "MP3" of the movie business.

French hacker, Jerome Rota, creates the first "DivX ;)" video codec, which is basically MP3 for videos. "DivX ;)" allows, in combination with DSL and other high-speed Internet access methods, users to share full movies via the Internet. Today, DivX is a company without the smiley in its name, with profits of approximately $84.9 million in 2007.

1998 - 2001

1998: The MP3 player.
The first portable MP3-player hits the shelves.

2000: Google gives up its ad-free policy.
By introducing Google Adwords, the company invents keyword advertising, a new form of online advertisement displaying relevant ads along with the search result. By 2009, Adwords is responsible for 95% of Google's income.

2000: Nobody can stop file sharing.
Napster is buried in lawsuits and is in danger of being forced to pay millions to labels. Yet, instead of this move decreasing file sharing, users jump to many other peer-2-peer tools such as Gnutella, eDonkey2000, Kazaa and Morpheus, which can now even share movies, e-books and software.

2000: The dotcom bubble.
The retained Internet hype starts blowing up in March 2000. The first stock prices go down and an increasing number of stocks are sold. Still, many investors believe the market will recover soon, and thus miss the right time to bail out, losing a fortune.

2001: The knowledge of the crowd: Wikipedia.
The free online encyclopedia, "Wikipedia", is founded and any Internet user is not only allowed to read Wikipedia articles for free, but he or she can also write or edit them. The days when people had to pay hundreds of Euros for a whole lexicon volume are over. Right now (September 2009), Wikipedia stores approximately 10 million articles provided in more than 230 languages.

2001 - 2003

2001: Apple launches iTunes.

Apple introduces iTunes and shows the music industry (with the "iTunes Music Store") how to make money by selling songs and albums via the Internet. By September 2006, Apple has sold more than 200 million songs in the USA and Canada. By the middle of 2007, Apple will have sold more than 3 billion songs, 50 million TV-series episodes and 2 million movies worldwide via "iTunes Store".

2001: Apple introduces the iPod.

In February, Jon Rubinstein introduces the first, 1.8-inch hard drive to Steve Jobs, along with the idea of carrying your whole music collection with you in your pocket. Steve Jobs says: "Go for it!" and on October 23rd, Apple presents the first iPod, featuring a 5 GB hard drive.

2003: Hello MySpace.

Tom Anderson founds the "MySpace" Internet community, and thus, re-defines the way all following generations communicate. In the future, some will meet their boyfriend or wife-to-be, not in a disco, but via a social network. In 2006, the 100th millionth member will get registered, and by the end of 2008, the number of members will have grown to 260 million.

2003 - 2004

2003: Skype scares the telecommunication industry.
Skype is Voice-over-IP software, which allows making calls or even video calls for free over the Internet. The beta version goes live in 2003. VoIP tools such as Skype jeopardize the core business of many telecommunication enterprises and cell phone service providers, since they are trying for a few more years to make money through telephone fees. The consequence will be that in 2009, cell phone service providers are doing their utmost to block the usage of Skype on their cell phones.

2004: UMTS makes the mobile web usable.
UMTS allows far higher data transfer rates than before. Finally, the way has been cleared for services such as mobile Internet, IPTV and Voice-over-IP services like Skype, which are going to become standard on every smart phone in just a few years from now.

2004: Competition for MySpace.
In February, Harvard student Mark Zuckerberg develops the social online network "Facebook" for his fellow students.

2004: World of Warcraft enters the market.
World of Warcraft, WoW in short, is an online role-playing game. Today, more than 11 million players are going online as dwarves and company, and are paying on a regular basis.

2005 - 2006

2005: Murdoch buys MySpace.
The media mogul, Rupert Murdoch, buys MySpace for $580m.

2005: Broadcast yourself.
Chad Hurley, Steve Chen and Jawed Karim found the Internet portal, "YouTube", on which users can upload and watch video clips for free.

12. October 2005: Goodbye video rental store.
The change doesn't stop at the doors of video rental stores. In October 2005, Apple presents the new video feature on iTunes. One year later, 550 TV shows and 75 movies can be downloaded in the USA. It's more than obvious that an increasing number of people can't be bothered to go outside and head for the next video rental store, since you can watch nearly any movie by simply clicking on it.

2006: Boom of the online travel agencies.
Another industry has changed utterly, which is the travel and tourism industry, since its core business has increasingly shifted to the Internet. Up until a few years ago, families flipped through brochures at travel agency offices and were looking for personal advice. Now, in 2006, an estimated 70 million people go online to gather information about their next holiday trip.

2006

2006: Google buys YouTube.

Google announces the take-over of YouTube for $1.5 billion.

2006: Facebook opens up.

Until September 2006, only American pupils, students and company employees were able to register with Facebook. From now on, students of foreign universities can also register.

2006: The first party for the digital natives.

On January 1st, 2006, the pirate party is founded in Sweden and becomes the first party to commit itself to civil and freedom rights as well as to freedom of information and data privacy. Its most important target groups are Internet users and file sharing platform users, deploying tools such as BitTorrent and students in particular.

2006: Internet changes the porn industry.

From the very beginning, pornography was one of the main drivers of the Internet and the word "sex" was one of the most often-entered terms in search engines. Yet, just as the high supply of freely available music caused big trouble for the music industry, the oversupply of sex on the net and Internet sites such as YouPorn (featuring free titty clips) made the conventional porn industry lose up to 50% of its income.

2006 - 2007

2006: The world starts tweeting.
The social network, "Twitter", is presented to the public in March 2006. Twitter is a so-called "micro blogging service". As with common blogs, it is mostly used as a public diary – the only difference being that it is fed in real-time via the cell phone, the web or several different apps and widgets, in never more than 140 characters. The purposes for which Twitter is being used are manifold. The NASA, for instance, has Twitter feeds for several of their projects; some Tweets even came in from outer space. The Los Angeles Fire Department will use this service for spreading information during the Southern California forest fires in 2007. Due to their short message character limit, notes on current events can often be found even faster on Twitter than on media backed up by editorial departments. Examples will be the emergency landing of US Airways flight 1549 or the Winnenden gun rampage.

October 2006: Suicide through MySpace
Megan M. commits suicide after being mobbed by a friend's mother through MySpace messages.

March 2007: Google Books starts scanning the world's literature.
Google has digitalised more than one million books. Nearly one-and-a-half years later, by October 2008, you will be able to flip through 7 million books on Google Books.

2007 - 2008

2007: The iPhone.

On June 29th, 2007, the first iPhone is available on the US market and is responsible for a drastic increase of mobile Internet usage. Already two years later, more than 65% of all mobile Internet users in the US go online with an iPhone or an iPod Touch.

2007: Radiohead says "Pay what you want".

Radiohead releases their album, "In Rainbows" as a digital download on their website and let every downloader pay as much as he or she wants – even nothing. Only in the first 29 days after the release, more than 1.2 million people visited the site and paid an average of $2.26 for the album. Twelve percent even paid between $8 and $12 - about the same amount like iTunes would charge.

2008: With the Internet strategy into the White House.

Thanks to a groundbreaking election strategy with the Internet and social websites such as MySpace and Facebook being its center point, Obama's campaign starts off with only 21 million dollars in May 2007 but is able to collect over 150 million dollars by September 2008 through small donations made via the Internet. Thanks to the "Neighbor-to-Neighbor" tool on My.BarackObama.com, Obama's supporting volunteers are able to reach far more people within their community in much less time than before. This selective deployment of e-mails, text messages and the support of the Obama girl in 2007 not only turn him into the most innovative, but also the "hippest" president.

2008 - 2010

2008: 1 out of 8 couples getting married in the USA have met online.

2008: Monty Python open their own YouTube channel to "suppress the illegal distribution of their videos". What appeared to be a typical Python joke at first quickly pays off for the guys: from then on the only way Monty Python DVDs know in the Amazon sales charts is up.

2009: Dell announces to have made more than 3 million dollars in computer sales via Twitter posts in 2007.

2009: More than 15,000 people in the newspaper industry have lost their jobs.

2010: Pope Benedict XVI calls on using the Internet even more than before to spread the "Word of Christ". Amen.

2009:
Media spending for ads in newspapers

-18%

Media spending for ads on TV

-10%

2009:
Media spending for mobile ads

+18%

Media spending for online ads

+9%

AND WHAT SHOULD I DO?

In order to stay relevant as a marketing professional, you now have to change the way you think. The following pages present 49 learnings that can help you make the move into the digital era of awesomeness.

Read, think about it, criticize, adopt what you like and build your own opinion. These are our personal experiences expressed in written words and do not represent the views of our past or current employers.

GOOD TO KNOW FOR YOURSELF:

Digital
is not a job
for specialists
anymore.

There will always be media specific specialists. Yet, nobody should take this as an excuse to do nothing. Nowadays, everybody should have an understanding of what digital is all about, be it a writer, a designer, an event manager, an accounter or a planner. Still, digital specialists themselves need to open up to traditional media and story telling, since theoretically, anyone must be able to take over the other person's job. An on-line writer should be able to write a TV script, just like the art director should know how to design a website.

In order to be able to solve problems of the future, any-one needs to have an understanding of the medium with which others on his or her team are working. If this is not the case, it is nearly impossible to create a truly integrated campaign, especially when separate departments are working as a team.

Lose the New Media Phobia.

You don't need to attend expensive seminars to learn how make use of New Media for yourself and your business. The best way to discover all the possibilities New Media have to offer is to live them. In short: Don't just read about it – do it. There are countless ways to start. If you don't have a Facebook account yet, get yourself one, find old friends, win new ones and cultivate them. Organize your weblinks, widgets and RSS feeds with Netvibes.com. Use Twitter.com to keep your friends updated in real-time. Go to Blogger.com and start your own blog. Get yourself a smart phone and discover the world of the apps. Create your own website by using one of hundreds of tools without needing to program one single line of code.

What's important is that you try things out for yourself and don't ask someone else to do them for you. By making your own experiences and mistakes, and having your very own little success stories, you will develop a better understanding and gain more self-confidence when talking to a client or a techie, since you will really know what you're talking about.

Make a Techi friend.

Ground-breaking technologies are going to be crucial parts of big campaigns in the future and already are. Yet, you can only develop campaigns with these if you know what's possible and what's not. Techies (some call them nerds) do know what's possible. Usually, they can be found under titles such as web developer, programmer, technical director or simply IT expert. Our techie at Jung von Matt was called "Mägic". He was a very kind nerd with the gift of being able to make other people understand complex processes and technologies. With a guy like this in the background, you can be relaxed from the very beginning and think of things as if anything was possible, letting him check afterwards whether things can be done the way you want them to be or not. If things turn out to be impossible until now, think of how they can be programmed or simply invent them to make them possible.

A continuous contact with your techie also provides you with new food for ideas and for understanding structures, something that, in turn, will help you with developing new ideas.

GOOD TO KNOW IN GENERAL:

Interactive doesn't mean it's digital.

Interactive doesn't automatically mean it must be a website, a banner campaign or something else like that. Interactivity should rather be the bar raised for all your ideas and campaigns. How can you make people interact with your advertisement, your TV spot or your integrated campaign? How can you integrate people in such a way that they become part of the campaign? What can you do to make them visit a website after stumbling over the respective print advertisement, and thus, to occupy themselves with the brand? How can you turn your campaign into a tool people keep using over and over again and tell their friends about? The times in which people just listened to a brand are over. A brand must give its users the possibility of interacting with it.

Bad example: Let's say we create an event that encourages people to lend their car to a friend for a test drive and the car brand rewards them for that. Now we could just send out flyers telling the people about the event and where they can sign up for it, but a better way might be to just create a Facebook application that does this job.

So, interactive doesn't mean it has to be digital. Digital media is simply often the best way to execute an interactive idea.

Integrate.
Don't interrupt.

In a time in which you can simply wipe away commercials with TiVO or download any movie you want from the Internet legally or illegally, commercials are increasingly avoided, both wanted or unwanted. People have understood that there are more than enough tools they can use to enjoy their movie (or whatever) without being interrupted by commercials.

So, a brand should draw attention towards itself without being considered a nuisance, but instead, an enrichment. Either it is integrated into the respective content or it creates a new one that people want to see. The digitalization of our environment is also a chance to think about new, maybe better ways of creating commercials. Maybe commercials could be customized and integrated into a TV show. So, for example, a billboard from a scene in the teeny show, "Gossip Girl", could be booked without creating any interruption; or brands could create tools around their products that can really help people accomplish things. So many opportunities: beautiful.

A brand should insert itself meaningfully into people's lives by enabling and enriching their existing behaviors, not by requiring new ones.

Having a blog is not enough.

Many CMO's are currently thinking of getting a blog, a YouTube channel, a Facebook group or an iPhone app for their products. The dangerous thing about this is that this advice alone is already considered by many to be a creative accomplishment. Many neglect to really make use of the respective medium channel and don't offer anything relevant to the user. So, instead of saying, "Let's have a blog" and then thinking about what you actually want to communicate through that blog, you should rather approach things the other way around. This means: Go and find some really relevant content you would like to communicate and then choose the best medium channel through which to address the desired people.

"If an idea doesn't work online, it's not a good idea."

One day, one of our ex-bosses said while talking to traditional creatives:

"If an idea doesn't work online, it's not a good idea."

He was right, because when you realize that your idea only works in a print ad or as a TV spot, it becomes obvious that this idea can't be that great. Of course, this quote also works the other way around. When an idea only works online or with a specific medium, it probably hasn't got enough relevance or potential to become an integrated campaign.

Every campaign is a global campaign.

Until a few years ago, the people had no idea of how a brand communicates in another country than his or her own. Yet today, we have the Internet. Everyone has it, everyone uses it, everything spreads at the speed of light, and above all, the Internet is global. So for example, when Volkswagen has launched a cool campaign for the USA, people in Germany will notice. Nowadays, companies keep losing an increasing amount of control over when, what and where people get to know about things.

Hence, when tossing something into the net, make sure it not only works for your country, but that it works for nearly anywhere else as well.

Focus on the individual.

In the past, people used to talk about target groups since it was impossible to address individuals. Yet through improved targeting, it is finally possible and will be accomplished in more diverse media.

The more people give insights into their lives on Facebook and such for free, enterprises like Google will track and store user behavior; the more possibilities there are to identify users, such as cookies, the larger the human database becomes that marketing people can access. This allows the creation of tailor-made advertisements and the ability to catch people at the best possible place.

This is why a "target group" suddenly becomes a "target person". It doesn't matter whether you like it or not: We know who you are, what you do, what you like and we can talk to you individually.

Yet these techniques are still very young, so right now, this intimate knowledge is recent. Although, think ten years in the future; then we have known you already for 10 or 15 years and have seen you growing up, changing and evolving – not only you, but also your entire social network.

The
Social Filter.

The more people use Twitter and other similar applications, the more that news will suddenly find its way to your desktop or your cell phone. Since you only follow people who are relevant to you, only news that are interesting to you will arrive on your desktop. What is created here is a social filter. In former times, an editor made the decision regarding which news was important for you and which not; now your social network is doing this job. Further, you determine who is part of that network.

So, the more people receive their individual news via social filters automatically, the less people will actively look for current information, since the information they want is suddenly just there.

The possible consequence for news portals is that the number of returning readers will drop, since people don't visit NYtimes.com that often anymore to flip through the headlines for relevant information. Rather, they pick up news from many different sites through their social filters. Since your social filter "Peter" links to an article on Spiegel.de, filter "Michael" to a blog entry and filter "Susan" to a forum, you don't get your information from one single source, but from many different ones.

In order to get picked up with an article, a product or a campaign by a social filter, these items have to have a certain relevance for that filter. This relevance varies from filter to filter, of course, so there is no general rule to which you can adhere. Yet, it definitely helps to make content shareable and to deploy the Viral Test. This method checks a campaign's "virality" and will be looked at closer later in this book.

Lies have long Tweets.

In the movie "Thank you for smoking" the spokesman of the tobacco industry tells his son about his job and says:

"When you argue right, you're never wrong."

This means with the right line of arguments, you could sell nearly anything, be it credit cards right in the middle of a financial crisis or burgers to fat Americans.

Thanks to the Internet this doesn't work that easily anymore. One example is the "Kryptonite" brand. The bicycle lock brand's slogan was:

'UNBREAKABLE BONDS'

It was bad luck for the company that a video appeared on the net showing how some of these locks could be picked by using a standard pen.

When the product itself is of poor quality, even the best marketing campaign can't make up for it anymore. Since when a brand lies, if they know it or not, there will be someone in this world who will find out about it and spread the news via Twitter and Co to thousands of people within seconds. Thus, honesty is still king.

It doesn't cost anything to listen.

People talk. That's what they've always been doing. However now, they do this in public on blogs, in forums and social networks. They talk and they also talk about brands. Even when actually many brands have realized, some are still afraid of criticism. Yet in most cases, it doesn't cost anything to just listen and maybe learn something important about your brand. The best thing would be to provide your brand with a platform of its own so people can tell you directly about the ideas, troubles and problems they have with your brand. After all, you can only win here.

People often make jokes about the "Web 2.0" trend and about someone launching his or her website as a "Beta" version. This is done to 1) have an excuse for small mistakes and 2) officially ask the people to send feedback – since it's not done yet and needs the help of all those testers out there.

One example for this just came from a friend and account guy. He had learned via Twitter that the website they had just launched still had some problems on certain browsers, and thus, was able to fix them in time before banners and TV spots made the traffic rise.

Apart from that, "listening" can help save money on expensive focus groups and spot dissatisfaction early.

Add meaning, not media.

We remember the launch of a compact car in Germany during which the whole country was covered with ads. We also believe this campaign to be one of the most expensive campaigns ever in Germany. Every corner had a picture of this small car standing in some dry desert. It was so much that people started making jokes about it, but funny enough, we no longer have any idea which car that was. The only thing we know is that it was a lot of ads and people got annoyed about this over-presence.

So don't push your product relying only on a large media budget, but rather, push it based on a cool idea. Since people won't get annoyed by that but will talk about it because they want to, the great media volume will generate nearly automatically – for far less money.

n the
media.

The value of your campaign is measured in contacts. Usually, there are three ways to gather contacts:

1. Paid media – These are media you pay for, be it an ad in a magazine or a banner on a website.
2. Press – Coverage of a product, event or campaign.
3. Word of mouth – People who tell their friends about a product or a campaign.

Now, there is a new way: **Owned media** – Media that belongs to a brand.

In former days, it was unthinkable that brands had their own media channels; but today, digitalization makes it easy and above all, affordable. The price for a print magazine can rise quickly, whereas calling up a website usually doesn't even cost a cent. This way, it is suddenly possible for brands to have their own media channel, from the funny microsite down to a complete brand community à la Nike.

In most cases, however, you need paid media, press and word of mouth, to draw people's attention towards owned media. Yet then owned media provide a means to bind and keep these people. So, points 1-3 are of a temporary character, whereas owned media is constant. Where paid media, press and word of mouth work rather like a sieve (one goes in and out again, just a few stay), owned media are the collecting basin to keep all those purchased contacts.

GOOD TO KNOW ABOUT TECHNOLOGY:

Using an innovative technology doesn't make an innovative idea.

As soon as an innovative technology appears on the web, it usually takes only a couple of months and three agencies have created an ad for award shows based on that new technology. Still, making use of innovative technologies doesn't automatically mean the basic idea behind it is innovative, too. In most cases, the only fascinating part of the ad is the technology itself.

So, do not start off with a great technology and then look for ideas, but rather, focus on a great idea first and then look for the right technology to bring this idea to life.

Technology has to serve the people.

People have always wanted to express themselves, to present themselves, to talk with each other and to play. The evolution of technology merely developed tools supporting people in unfolding these deeply rooted needs. Yet, it has not reinvented people's behaviors, but only developed them further.

Technology should be adapted to people's habits and make things easier. I feel like playing and turn on my XBox. I feel like presenting myself and thus create a website. I feel like I want to know what my friends are doing today and read their status messages on Facebook.

Technology is deployed right, when it's invisible.

At the E3 2009, the world's largest trade show for electronic entertainment, Microsoft presented project Natal: An XBox controller that is able to recognize gestures and speech, and thus allows you to control games and other content on your TV screen without a remote control or the physical contact with other kinds of controllers. This is only possible through a complex interplay of different technologies, but still, the user doesn't realize this. You don't have to press buttons on fancily designed devices; you simply act intuitively.

This means technology is deployed in a right way when the user doesn't realize it's there, when he's doing something without thinking about what he is doing and simply does what he's used to doing.

"Things are only impossible until they are not."

- Jean-Luc Picard

Sometimes it's a good thing to only have half-knowledge, since many "onliners" have such a profound knowledge about technology that they tend to only think about what they know really works. It can be an advantage to keep a certain degree of naïveté, since that way, you can think freely, at a larger scale and not only about what's possible, but something like, "Wouldn't it be cool if ...". As long as you haven't tried everything to make it possible, it's still not impossible. As Star Trek's Jean-Luc Picard once put it:

"Things are only impossible until they're not."

GOOD TO KNOW FOR YOUR IDEAS:

Focus on one.

Especially when thinking about ideas for websites, one gets easily taken away by ideas and would rather integrate 200 great tools and ideas into one site. Yet, 200 great tools are, by far, not as overwhelming as ONE single really unbelievable top-notch idea.

As soon as someone wants to tell someone else about this site, he suddenly has to focus hard on telling about this whole bunch of ideas. The real, basic idea of the site can easily get lost. So, look at which of these 200 ideas really is the best of all and make this one idea really great, top-notch and overwhelming, since this single idea is easier to talk about than 200.

Don't get us wrong here; an integrated campaign can consist of many smaller ideas, but each one of these ideas must be able to stand by itself. This means: In the case of web ideas, each idea should have its own websites, e-mail or app and should not be hidden among many others.

three types of integrated campaigns.

Many companies and agencies still believe that an additional website and banner ad turn their traditional campaign automatically into an integrated campaign. Over the last few years, we have formed our own opinion on this and have spotted three different types of integrated campaigns.

1. The adaptive campaign

Let's say you have an idea for a great TV spot, for instance. Now you think of how this TV spot could look like printed, as a banner ad and as a website. Still basically, each execution is the same. This may make every execution very recognizable, but also lame. There is a reason why you get annoyed when you see the same TV commercial four times in a row. Many creatives already call this an "integrated campaign", but we would rather call this an "adaptive campaign".

2. The integrated campaign

You have a medium-independent idea based on an insight that suits your brand or product. Based on this idea, you come up with concepts for all required campaign media (TV, print, web, out of home, etc.). Compared with the adaptive campaign, the individual media display the campaign idea in their very own way. Here, each campaign component has its own idea, tailor-made to fit the respective medium.

So, let's say your campaign idea is "Deals so good, happiness is hard to hide". Here, the TV spot shows people who are unable to bargain anymore, since they can't manage to suppress their joy. Online, you can hire a virtual "dealer" to negotiate on your behalf on Craigslist etc. No award winner here, but you get the point. ➔

The three types of integrated campaigns./2

The result: People discover and experience more and more with each campaign component, but perceive the overall campaign as one whole, integrated experience. This is, for us, the basic version of an integrated campaign.

3. Integrated campaign with event character
You have a medium-independent idea that feels already press worthy without any execution. Based on this idea, which is usually of an event nature, creating TV spots, banner ads or funny Facebook apps comes easy. A good example for this would be Crispin's Coke Zero campaign.

The idea: "Coke Zero" tastes like Coke; that's why Coke sues "Coke Zero" and thus, basically themselves. On TV, real-life reactions of lawyers on this were shown and online you were able to sue your friends for the same taste.

Other good examples are the "The Best Job in the World" campaign in which you were able to win the job of your dreams of becoming a paid inhabitant of an Australian island, or Burger King's "Whopper Freakout" campaign in which the Whopper disappeared from the menu for one day to prove the people's love for the burger by showing their reactions.

In a best case scenario, the campaign always leads to a brand platform to keep the conversation going, even when the campaign is over – even if the platform is just a Twitter account. We believe this to be the master class of an integrated campaign.

Viral is not YouTube.

Many friends of ours in the industry tell us about their bosses briefing them on viral campaigns, but in the end, all they have in mind is a funny and provocative video on YouTube.

But what really is a viral campaign?

A viral campaign is content that is so good or is optimized towards a current momentum that people voluntarily tell others about it.

Which brings us to the point that viral campaigns don't necessarily have something to do with digital media, because the goal of a campaign like this is to make people talk about your brand or your product.

During the financial crisis, there was a campaign by Hyundai that gave people the guarantee that if they lose their job the following year, Hyundai would buy their car back. It was an idea that spread virally without solely living online.

During the past years, digital media have pushed viral ideas even more, because now you can track live how many people have told their friends about them. Viral essentially became measurable. Suddenly, marketing people became aware that their money was able to accomplish much more than just buying fixed contacts.

This is a great thing. However, one should not forget that the kick-off for a viral campaign doesn't necessarily need to take place online. All it needs to be is an idea people like telling others about.

Don't plan to be viral. Plan to be awesome.

Can I plan my campaign in such a way that it is viral? Yes, by doing something that is really amazingly overwhelmingly awesome. Everything that is really amazingly overwhelmingly awesome becomes viral automatically, because everyone enjoys sending his or her friends something that is really amazingly overwhelmingly awesome.

That's for sure.

By the way, you can often read that this or that company has "launched a viral campaign the other day," although it is impossible to launch a viral campaign, since a campaign only becomes viral if it gets forwarded by the people.

The Viral Test.

One thing we have learned at CP+B is what we like to call "the Viral Test". When do you know that the idea you have is really awesome? When it is talked about in the media, since the best ad is the one people like telling others about and which is so good that the media think it's worthwhile giving coverage to it.

Hence this tip: As soon as you have an idea, write it down in the same way the media would write on it. If that works out well, your idea is probably really viral and is likely to be talked about in the media and by the people.

So take the Viral Test and ask yourself:

"Is my idea worth writing about?"

Do it for real.

If you want your idea to pick up steam and generate media coverage, you should simply imagine people's response. The best would be:

"Holy shit! They really did this!?"

If this is the response you want to get, there is a simple rule to follow:

Do it for real.

Burger King really fed people who had never seen a Burger in their life with the Whopper. 7Eleven have really re-built their stores into Quick-e-Marts. The Swedish agency, ACNE, has really thrown an oversized dice down a glacier and had people bet on the outcome.

All these campaigns have received intense media coverage. Why? Because it was no fake; they did it for real.

The
Forced Viral.

Of course things do not become viral just like that. They need selected "injections", postings on blogs, press releases etc. The content needs to be pushed. Yet with certain actions, you can turn people into multipliers. Before downloading this book for free, people get asked to post a Tweet on it, for instance. Another idea would be to first tell three friends about it before being allowed to download it.

But a Forced Viral doesn't necessarily have to do with free content. As soon as an action deals with social stuff, this task is taken on automatically. Taking Whopper Sacrifice from Burger King as an example, as soon as you delete one of your friends on Facebook for a Whopper, the friend is automatically informed about your action via that app and this draws his or her attention automatically towards it. An automated, pre-programmed virality evolves.

Give it a name.

For TV spots, having a name was only important when they were entered in award shows in order to once again emphasize the basic idea behind the spot. However, today when campaigns often are full events spanning across different media, having a name is more important than ever before. When someone notices the campaign, what's the way the viewer tells his or her friends about it?

"Hey Dude! Have you seen the campaign where people just get crazy 'cause they don't get a Whopper? Gotta' google that one!"

Or

"Hey Dude! Have you already seen the Whopper Freakout? It's on WhopperFreakout.com"

So, a good, catchy name can help you with two things:
1. It can help you pass on the information.
2. It can help identify the domain or for finding the campaign easily online as soon as you've heard about it.

And when you have done everything right, the name might even be incorporated in people's vocabulary.

Serve the On-Demand-Society.

Along with the proceeding digitalization of our environment and the spreading of the Internet, our society has increasingly changed into an on-demand society, as people become more and more accustomed to things being available right away. Your complete music collection in your pocket, any video clip can be reached with just a few clicks on YouTube and 24/7 grocery stores. Having to wait has never been as painful as it is today. When the video doesn't load within seconds, people tend to freak out.

As a result, we were able to watch live as business models based on on-demand grew rapidly during the past few years. By 2009, iTunes, for instance, had sold more than 6 million songs since its launch in 2003 – and it's no wonder. When someone listens to music today, it is digitalized, which means when I go and buy myself a CD, I not only have to wait until I'm back home, I also have to rip it onto my mp3-player to be able to listen to it on the go.

Make it accessible.

When Napster was released in 1999 (or rather, popped up), it struck a chord with people.

Chord one:
"Fuck! I can download any song and burn it on CD!!!"

Chord two:
"How awesome! I can leech the music I want, whenever I want!!!"

You can't do much about the "chord one" people since there will always be ways to download music illegally from the web. Sometimes it will be easy, sometimes not so easy, but it will always be possible. "Chord one", however, is crucial for today's on-demand society. Here, Napster has met a need no one has ever met before.

In April 2003, four years after Napster was launched, iTunes Music Store was opened in the States and finally met the need of being able to buy music whenever people felt like it – but this time, it was all safe and legal. Since those people who didn't dare to download illegally and were afraid of getting caught now bought their music from iTunes, only when these people don't find their music on iTunes, they might go back to file sharing. ➔

Make it
accessible./2

This is like at a grocery store. If I don't find the choco-late bar I've seen being advertised all week long at my local store, I go and buy a different one, or I just don't buy anything.

The result: In an on-demand society, companies have to make sure that their products are as available as they can be, which means via a variety of channels. When a user can't get his or her need met immediately the user will wander off to the competition, be it a legal or an illegal one.

ke it
mixable.

In times when anyone is able to produce an album or an entire movie on his or her home computer, the remix has become a tool more than ever before to not only let unfold someone's creativity but also to express someone's opinion in the form of a parody or a collage. This can be done through sound, vision or many other interactive forms you can think of.

Remix has become part of communication. People use it to present their opinion quickly without boring others, be it in a positive or a negative way. The coming generation is not a pure society of users anymore but a society of producers. It has grown up creating and distributing its own content. A product or a campaign it cannot interact with is simply irrelevant for that generation. Hence, it is crucial that your product or your campaign is not only interactive, but also "remixable".

Some wise man once said:

"Getting spoofed is the biggest praise you can get."

Any parody usually needs a discussion going on beforehand. The best thing that can happen to someone is to trigger a discussion, since suddenly, people occupy themselves with a product or a campaign and the number of your contacts multiplies automatically.

Make it shareable.

In May 2009, one of the first phishing schemes (a way to gather user data illegally) on Facebook made the rounds. People received a message from a friend saying "Hey! Check www.xyz.com". After clicking on that link a page would open up looking exactly like the Facebook page, asking for a username and a password. It seemed to be quite normal, because sometimes you have to login once again. Yet now the phishing guys had your Facebook account data, and the first thing they did with your data was send messages to even more friends of yours in your name. The point was that the reason that these phishing messages were so successful was that people had blind trust in that link – just because it was "recommended" by a friend. This is a good example for how much people trust their friends.

The opinion of friends has always been something on which people relied. Today, this opinion is spread via status messages. So, nowadays, one of the best things that can happen to a product is to find its way into a status message on Facebook, Twitter and the like. That's why it is crucial to make your product or your campaign as shareable as possible, since the easier people can post it on Facebook and such, the more likely that product or campaign gets recommended to others.

Use the power of the status message.

One of our Creative Directors has just posted on Facebook:

"Good morning, LA"

Without haven spoken a single word with him, I know that he's in L.A. right now. A status message on Facebook or Twitter is able to give me full knowledge of what's going on in the everyday life of someone I know. I can read where he or she currently is, what he's interested in or simply what's bothering him.

The status message is the social megaphone of the digital generation. All you have to do is type in a few characters and the message is sent to the desktops of all your friends. While we distributed funny videos via e-mail a few years ago, this is done through our status message today.

The interesting thing is that everybody is concerned about data privacy on the Internet, whereas nearly everybody "undresses" himself willingly. We're still waiting for the news message that someone broke into someones's house because he or she had twittered to be on holiday.*

For marketing people like us, status messages are of particular importance since they work basically like a personal recommendation. Also, in the future, more and more automated tools will be connected with them. So, one day the news that I've just entered Star-bucks might do the rounds as soon as I set my foot on their doorstep – fully automated, to all my friends.

* Note: While making the last changes of our book, we hear of a gang in Beverly Hills that broke into several celebrity homes and stole a multitude of diamonds. They only were able to do so,because they always knew when the celebrities were out of town – thanks to their updated Twitter feeds.

Become
personal.

Name three websites you visit every day. I bet you visit at least two of these websites out of a personal interest, such as YouTube or Social Networking. This is in addition to the piles of e-mails and all the content linked on Facebook and the like. All in all, this is certainly more content that is of a personal interest to you than content that is job related.

So how can a product or a campaign become personal content? The best thing would be to provide something that integrates with your personal life, such as Nike Plus. Here, a brand interferes with your personal experience of jogging and you even think that's cool.

One option any brand has are Facebook apps, be it different kinds of personality tests, deleting your friends for a Whopper or your personal love song combined with a slideshow of pictures of shared moments. Facebook is the perfect place to become part of the personal content millions of people consume every day, since as soon as a brand engages your personal information or your friends, it automatically becomes personal content.

So, one of the requirements an idea should have is that the campaign itself is already able to create personal moments, because then, your idea becomes socially relevant to people and they will start talking about it.

Everyone is a reporter.

On January 15th, 2009, Janis K. tweeted:

"There's a plane in the Hudson. I'm on the ferry going to pick up the people. Crazy."

His tweet probably was the first public message on that event. A picture he had attached to his tweet was later used by the press. That message came from an individual person and not from a news company.

New Media, with the speed and interconnectedness they have, can be used by a single person to have nearly as much power as a gigantic news corporation has. The outcome is that people will be the first ones in many cases and press will lose its monopoly position in terms of informational edge. Eyewitnesses suddenly turn into authors and report directly, without any detours, ignoring the press. The press quotes later on.

Hence, engage people – because in most cases, they will be there before you.

The biggest German daily newspaper, the BILD, has realized this already a few years ago and has thus created the "BILD Leser-Reporter" (BILD reader reporter). You see something you think is newsworthy? Take a picture or a video with your cell phone, send it exclusively to BILD and when they print it you will get a few Euros.

Exceed expectations.

In America there's an online store for shoes, Zappos. com. The way this store is designed is horrible and I was concerned about my credit card data when I ordered there. Only 12 minutes after I placed my order, however, I received an e-mail that it was dispatched, that they wouldn't charge delivery costs and that they would even upgrade to overnight delivery since they appreciate having me as a customer. 10 hours later, I had my new shoes on my feet and I'm so happy that everything went so smoothly that I even write about it in a book and do promotion for these guys – and all they had done was exceed my expectations.

So, it is important as a company to not only talk about how to meet the customers' expectations, but also to think of how these can even be exceeded. This is especially true because through New Media, a quick Google search is able to completely change your buying decision. Today, it's not about what a single friend thinks, but what thousands of users think.

Update: Meanwhile, Zappos has been bought by Amazon – for $928,000,000.

Dope your products digitally.

The beautiful thing about advertising is that nearly anything is allowed. Even doping. From smoking weed at the Christmas party down to doping products this chapter is about.

So, the New Media have made doping products easy, and above all, affordable. Almost any product can have a digital extension now. A nice example: When you go and buy a Kinder Surprise Egg, you not only find a toy inside but also a code for an online game.

All of a sudden, digital media enable you to have influence on the product without having to influence the product itself, since digital extensions are cheap and open new ways for improving a product.

Give your story a simple idea.

Let's briefly take a look at the movie industry. This is also a topic that can be used for making concepts for a campaign.

Name a porn movie you know the title of and the story line. 70% of the people reading this will probably think about Deep Throat from the 70s. Meanwhile, 20% really watch a lot of porn movies while 10% couldn't even name one.

But why was Deep Throat so much more successful than other porn movies? It had a clear, simple idea – an idea that can easily be told to others and a storyline that follows that idea all along. That means when you think of that movie, you don't really think about the story but the concept idea: Girl realizes her clitoris is in her throat and you can already guess how the rest of the story goes.

Another good example is the Saw series. Each year, a new film is released doing nothing more than moving from torture trap to torture trap, and each year, that movie is another smasher.

So when a story contains a simple idea, it can easily be told to others, and the story itself can be continued easily as well.

Banners are the new print ads.

Many creative heads have prejudices against banner ads, since the only thing they have in mind when they hear the term are flashing pop-ups. While print ads always used to be the medium that gave proof of one's creative excellence, online banners are becoming the place to really be creative.

You have to keep in mind that banner ads are, at best, interactive and thus open up many more possibilities for being creative than a print ad does. Movies, games, music, social media and all kinds of possible effects turn the banner into a creative playground in pixel dimensions.

So don't be afraid of banner ads, but rather consider them as a chance to produce really hot shit capable of winning awards.

GOOD TO KNOW IN GENERAL: PART 2

Buying doesn't mean you own it.

In July 2009, Amazon had a quarrel with the publishing house of George Orwell's classic, 1984. It seemed that a Kindle version of the book (eBook version by Amazon) was put up for sale on Amazon.com without any agreements made beforehand. Amazon's response was simple and quite efficient: Stopping the sale immediately and deleting that eBook from all Kindle devices. Yes, they've deleted it. "But the people had already bought the book," some of you might think. Yet, in a world of digital interconnectedness, buying something does not automatically mean you own it. Since a Kindle, Amazon's eBook reader, updates automatically with the online shop, the result is that Amazon has total control of which content is stored on the devices and which is not. Things are quite similar with the iTunes store and theoretically also with data stored on the iPhone. With a simple update, Apple could get full control over your iTunes and iPhone data.

That was a real gift for the press, of course, since it was 1984, a novel about the state having total control over its citizens. Amazon gave all buyers of the book a voucher of the same value and released an official apology in which they stated that things like that would never ever happen again. ➔

Buying doesn't mean you own it./2

What do we learn from this?

1. Digitalization means more control. The question is who has the control, since when I make use of a service I can use to lock my home door with while traveling, this means more control for me. On the other hand, that service will also be able to open my door anytime, too.

2. In a digital world, buying something does not mean you own it. When Amazon takes away a book from you, a book you've bought, this would be stealing – right?

Use the crowd.

At the time we're writing this book, crowdsourcing has become one of the most popular buzzwords. So what actually is crowdsourcing? Wikipedia says:

"Crowdsourcing is a neologistic compound of Crowd and Outsourcing for the act of taking tasks traditionally performed by an employee or contractor, and outsourcing them to a group of people or community, through an "open call" to a large group of people (a crowd) asking for contributions."

So, the idea is outsourcing onto the intelligence of other people, for free, if possible. This is actually exactly what Google is doing, since most of the Google products are not based on a content of their own, but on the content of others (YouTube, Google Search, Google Books etc.) Yet Google adapts to the on-demand society, because they make this content immediately available to anyone.

With crowdsourcing, it's also about creating tools that can help companies listen to what their users want or what they don't want as well as give people the opportunity to contribute to the brand. The Apple App Store, for instance, is crowdsourcing at its best. Here, thousands of free developers voluntarily work on software exclusively for Apple products, the iPhone, iPod and iPad. They do this without Apple paying them. Of course, these developers get their share of the sales, but at their own risk; the apps they've programmed either pay off or they don't. Apart from that, each new app increases the value of the iPhone and Co and provides an additional reason for people to buy it.

User-Gen needs guidance.

Nowadays, creative content in the sense of entertainment, advertisement and journalism is created by more than a small elitist circle of creatives behind closed doors during long brainstorming sessions. The Internet has opened the doors wide and all are invited to contribute and upload to YouTube or to post on Facebook.

Still, creatives in marketing don't need to be afraid of losing their jobs, since leaving everything to the users would only end up in anarchy. Yet when a brand decides to carry through a user-gen campaign, it's crucial not to give the users too much freedom. The more means, specifications and tools to which the users get to contribute with their creativity, the easier it's going to be for them, the more people are going to participate and the better the result will be.

The Freemium Model.

The philosophy the first Internet users had was that any piece of information should be available immediately and for free, to anyone, anytime. The web community is accustomed to getting content for free, be it music, movies, books and of course, information of any kind.

Theoretically, any type of digital goods can be provided for free on the Internet, since digital goods can be multiplied endlessly without losing quality and at very low costs.

When you release a new service or a new product online, it makes sense, at the beginning at least, to give it away for free. Since the web community has grown up with getting things for free, it will accept your new product with open arms and will spread it voluntarily, since costs without trying it first usually repel Internet users. When the free basic version keeps what it promised, many users will then be willing to pay for the premium version of that service or product. If it's not you who provides it for free, someone else is going to do it. So this is also part of competitiveness.

We have pinched the term 'Freemium' from Chris Anderson. The Wired magazine chief editor has written a whole book on this topic. The author even keeps his promise, since you can get his book Free online, for free. Just google it.

The $9.900 elf.

More than 11.5 million users are playing the World of Warcraft online role-playing game. An account costs at least $11 every month. So this makes a turnover of approximately $126.5m every month. That's not bad for something that's supposed to be a niche product – not to speak of trading with virtual goods and high-level characters from the game on eBay and the like. In September 2007, for instance, a World of Warcraft account with a high-level character was sold for £5,000 (approximately $9,900 at that time).

Another phenomenon is Farmville. Farmville is currently the most popular Facebook application. In this game, it's about building your own farm. The more you play, the farther you get and the more virtual money you get with which to buy great new goodies. In October 2009, that game had more than 56,1m active (!) users. It started in June of the same year. By making use of forced viral tactic, it got 5 times as many active users as World of Warcraft has within four months. This is because when you are successful in the game, the news is posted on your Facebook wall and all your friends will notice. If you want to get new goodies faster, you can also buy them for real dollars.

For the digital generation, virtual goods sometimes have nearly as much value as real goods, since they build up a personal relation with their game or tool over time. That's why it's worth looking from time to time at which digital goods your tool can have, since they may turn into another income source in the future.

Piracy pushes innovation.

Internet piracy is a crime, no doubt about that. But why are these crimes not seen as what they are by a whole generation?

These people have grown up with a technology that provided them with new ways of consuming and trading content. The new ways had suddenly met a need that was always there – being able to enjoy music and movies whenever people felt like it.

A few years after the first file-sharing networks revolutionized the Internet and high-speed connections like DSL allowed watching movies in real-time, smart companies have realized that it made no sense to suppress people's needs; instead, they thought of ways to make profit with these needs. This is one reason why iTunes and Hulu entered the market.

Today, many TV broadcasting companies put their series online so they can be watched for free instead of suing sites that have done this before they did. So, don't go and look at whom you can sue, but rather try and find out how to meet unsatisfied needs – to make profit.

Neo-mobilization.

When Mahmoud Ahmadinejad was re-elected president in Iran and was accused of election fraud, thousands of demonstrators gathered via Twitter and similar services.

During the election in the US, Obama's campaign team provided a platform for the people they could use to mobilize themselves in order to stage their own election events.

Another younger case of neo-mobilization took place at the end of 2009 in the UK. Since people were fed up with the winner of the last casting show always leading the British charts around Christmas, a Facebook group called out on boycott. Due to the line, "Fuck you I won't do what you tell me," that year the 17 year-old song "Killing in the Name" by Rage Against The Machine was supposed to be the chart leader. So, everyone was called to buy the single by this American Metal band to prevent that year's winner of the casting show ("X-Factor"), Joe McElderry, from becoming number 1 in the charts. Then, right on time for Christmas, the number 1 of the British charts was announced; the Christmas single for 2009 in the UK was Rage Against the Machine with "Killing in the Name", with more than 500,000 sold singles – 50,000 more than Joe McElderry's "The Climb".

What does that mean: The Internet enables people to get themselves mobilized in no time, even when those people don't know each other.

The people will be always online.

It's 7:30am in the morning and John's cell phone alarm is ringing. His Twitter account automatically announces that he's getting up right now. He takes a shower, quickly shoves a slice of toast down his throat and leaves the house. From then on, his friends on Skype can see that he's online. Arriving at the subway station, he receives a message from his colleague:

"Ey John! I can see you're already on your way, I've overslept, keep me covered."

And John replies:
"Sure thing, Bill!"

Yet his train is late and he can watch the morning meeting starting off without him on his cell phone.

A few years back, people were asked in surveys how long they were online per week. Now, with smart phones, you are always online, because the smart phone always is. This means you're available anywhere at any time, not only for your friends, but also for receiving ad messages. What's more – via your GPS, we even know where you are and can contact you right on location.

Everything will be digital.

In 2007, seven countries started reconstructing their analogue TV into a digital signal. Many think of digital television only to get digital picture quality, such as HD TV. Yet digitalizing TV also has other great factors, such as tracking and targeting. That way, viewing rates will not only be defined by selected average citizens, but by every single viewer, since it can be precisely tracked who is watching for how long and what. In the next step, they even know who this person is. Another thing digitalization has in store is interactivity, and this will not only be the case with TV. Also, print media will become digital sooner or later, and thus, interactive. Amazon, for instance, is already pushing digital books right now – books that can be read with Amazon's own eBook reader, Kindle, anywhere. These are books that can also be bought anywhere. That way, people will buy books nearly always digitalized, just like music from the iTunes store.

As a traditional ad guy, you should get some experience in the digital field under your belt as quickly as possible, since sooner or later, everything will be digital and having experience in that field or not will be the deciding factor regarding your being hired or getting fired.

e End.
So far ...

Actually, what we witness today is just the beginning of the digital era of awesomeness. The new media are like a large Research and Development department in which countless new business models are tested every day. When you compare the sheer number of new media start-ups in general with the number of new media start-ups, which have received relevance in society or even make profit, you realize there is still no universal rule for success within the world of new media. Sometimes people try to make us believe the key for online success has been found by throwing out new insights, inventions and trends, such as "viral", "branded utilities", "social media" and now "crowdsourcing", but the potential of new media has not been reached by far. In fact, in the years to come, there is still a lot to discover and a lot to forget. (Do you remember Second Life?)

Because this is just the beginning.

P.S.: You can find all the case examples from the book at www.ohmygodwhathappened.com/cases

WHO THE FUCK ARE INNOVATIVE THUNDER?

Innovative Thunder is a creative team for innovative marketing solutions. Currently Thunder, alias Leif Abraham and Christian Behrendt, work as an Associate Creative Director team with AdWeek's Digital Agency of the Decade and the creators of Nike+, R/GA New York. Here, they create worldwide campaigns and platforms for brands like MasterCard and Nike.

Before that, Thunder was the Lead Interactive team at the Activision/Guitar Hero account with AdAge's Agency of the Decade, Crispin, Porter + Bogusky in Boulder, Colorado, where they created the launch campaign of the video game "DJ Hero". Apart from that, Thunder worked with CP+B for brands like Best Buy, Volkswagen and Burger King Germany. And because the job title of the 'Concept Creative' doesn't exist in the US, their business cards just said 'Innovative Thunder'.

Leif and Christian met at Germany's Hotshop Jung von Matt in Hamburg, where they created campaigns for brands such as Mercedes-Benz, Sixt rent a car and the TV series, Lost. With JvM alone, Thunder has won more than 90 national and international awards. They were part of the team that made Jung von Matt Worldwide Agency of the Year 2007 (The BigWon) as well as for the first time Interactive Agency of the Year 2007 and 2008 (Horizont). ➜

WHO THE FUCK ARE INNOVATIVE THUNDER?/2

Before his agency life Christian worked as a marketing manager for domestic and international Pop, Dance and Techno artists such as Peaches, Scooter and Brooklyn Bounce. Under Christian's supervision, Brooklyn Bounce became Sony Music/Germany's most successful national artist in 2001, a success for which he received a Gold Record. One year later, Christian became Head of Beat Department at Warner Music/Wea Germany. When the music industry's downturn started, he decided to pass his salary, sell his car and his apartment and move back to his parent's house in order to switch to another industry. He won a scholarship from the Miami Ad School and started after a successful graduation in 2005, his second career with Jung von Matt where he met Leif, and their joint creative romance began.

Leif created various Internet projects for several years, from one of Germany's biggest gaming networks with more than 8 million page impressions per month down to managing several affiliate marketing projects. Based on his experience and expertise on the digital field, Leif started off with Jung von Matt at the age of 19 and became the agency's youngest employee at the time.

Since 2010, Leif & Christian are teaching at the Miami Ad School, New York.

Sources

1969: The Internet is born.
http://de.wikipedia.org/wiki/Internet#Geschichte

1971: The first e-mail.
http://de.wikipedia.org/wiki/E-Mail#Geschichte

1983: The cell phone is invented.
1990: Accessing the Internet with your cell phone.
http://en.wikipedia.org/wiki/Mobile_phone
http://de.wikipedia.org/wiki/Mobiltelefon

1989: The WorldWideWeb is born.
http://de.wikipedia.org/wiki/World_Wide_Web
http://en.wikipedia.org/wiki/World_Wide_Web

1989: The invention of the MP3.
http://de.wikipedia.org/wiki/MP3#Geschichte
http://en.wikipedia.org/wiki/MP3

1988/90: DSL pushes the Internet.
http://de.wikipedia.org/wiki/Digital_Subscriber_Line#Geschichte

1993: The golden Shield.
http://en.wikipedia.org/wiki/Golden_Shield_Project#References

1993: The first CD burners hit the market.
http://de.wikipedia.org/wiki/Brenner_(Hardware)#Geschichte

1994: The first banner ads are sold.
http://en.wikipedia.org/wiki/Web_banner#History

1994/95: The foundation of Yahoo.
http://de.wikipedia.org/wiki/Yahoo#Unternehmensgeschichte

1997: Blank CDs enter the charts.
http://de.wikipedia.org/wiki/Musikindustrie#Krisen

1998: College Kid destroys the music industry.
http://de.wikipedia.org/wiki/Napster

1998: Google.
http://de.wikipedia.org/wiki/Google
http://en.wikipedia.org/wiki/Google_search

1998: The "MP3" of the movie business.
http://de.wikipedia.org/wiki/DivX
http://en.wikipedia.org/wiki/DivX#History

1998: The MP3 player.
http://de.wikipedia.org/wiki/MP3-Player

2000: Google gives up its ad-free policy.
http://en.wikipedia.org/wiki/AdWords

Sources/2

2000: Nobody can stop file sharing.
http://en.wikipedia.org/wiki/File_sharing

2000: The dotcom bubble.
http://de.wikipedia.org/wiki/Dotcom-Blase#Der_Absturz
http://en.wikipedia.org/wiki/Dotcom_boom#The_bubble_bursts

2001: The knowledge of the crowd: Wikipedia.
http://en.wikipedia.org/wiki/Wikipedia

2001: Apple launches iTunes.
http://de.wikipedia.org/wiki/ITunes#Geschichte
http://en.wikipedia.org/wiki/ITunes

2001: Apple introduces the iPod.
http://en.wikipedia.org/wiki/IPod
http://de.wikipedia.org/wiki/Apple_iPod

2003: Hello MySpace.
http://de.wikipedia.org/wiki/MySpace
http://en.wikipedia.org/wiki/MySpace

2003: Skype scares the telecommunication industry.
http://en.wikipedia.org/wiki/Skype#History

2004: UMTS makes the mobile web usable.
http://en.wikipedia.org/wiki/Umts
http://de.wikipedia.org/wiki/Universal_Mobile_Telecommunications_System

2004: Competition for MySpace.
http://de.wikipedia.org/wiki/Facebook

2004: World of Warcraft enters the market.
http://de.wikipedia.org/wiki/World_Of_Warcraft

2005: Murdoch buys MySpace.
http://en.wikipedia.org/wiki/MySpace

2005: Broadcast yourself.
http://en.wikipedia.org/wiki/Youtube

12. October 2005: Goodbye video rental store.
http://en.wikipedia.org/wiki/ITunes

2006: Boom of the online travel agencies.
http://en.wikipedia.org/wiki/Online_travel_agency

2006: Google buys YouTube.
http://de.wikipedia.org/wiki/YouTube

2006: Facebook opens up.
http://de.wikipedia.org/wiki/Facebook

006: The first party for the digital natives.
http://de.wikipedia.org/wiki/Piratenparteien#Geschichte

2006: Internet changes the porn industry.
http://de.wikipedia.org/wiki/Youporn
http://en.wikipedia.org/wiki/YouPorn

2006: The world starts tweeting.
http://en.wikipedia.org/wiki/Twitter

October 2006: Suicide through MySpace
http://en.wikipedia.org/wiki/MySpace_Suicide_Case

March 2007: Google Books starts scanning the world's literature.
http://en.wikipedia.org/wiki/Google_Books

2007: The iPhone.
http://en.wikipedia.org/wiki/Iphone

2007: Radiohead says "Pay what you want".
http://en.wikipedia.org/wiki/Radiohead

2008: With the Internet strategy into the White House.
http://de.wikipedia.org/wiki/Barack_Obama#Rolle_des_Internets

2008: 1 out of 8 couples getting married in the USA have met online.
http://www.youtube.com/watch?v=jpEnFwiqdx8&feature=related

2008: Monty Python open their own YouTube chan- nel to "suppress the illegal distribution of their vid- eos".
http://mashable.com/2008/11/19/monty-python-youtube/

2009: Dell announces to have made more than 3 million dollars in computer sales via Twitter posts in 2007.
http://www.youtube.com/watch?v=6ILQrUrEWe8&feature=related

2009: More than 15,000 people in the newspaper industry have lost their jobs.
http://news-cycle.blogspot.com/2009/12/more-than-15000-people-have-lost-their.html

2008: 1 out of 8 couples getting married in the USA have met online.
http://www.youtube.com/watch?v=jpEnFwiqdx8&feature=related

2010: Pope Benedict XVI calls on using the Inter- net even more than before to spread the "Word of Christ".
http://www.heise.de/newsticker/meldung/Papst-will-Internet-staerker-zur-Missionierung-nutzen-911799.html

Media spendings - page 42,43
http://www.youtube.com/watch?v=6ILQrUrEWe8&feature=related
http://www.nytimes.com/2009/08/04/business/media/04adco.html

Sources/4

"One example is the "Kryptonite" brand."
http://www.wired.com/culture/lifestyle/news/2004/09/64987
http://en.wikipedia.org/wiki/Kryptonite_lock

Serve the on-demand society
http://en.wikipedia.org/wiki/Itunes

Page 129:
Janus K.'s tweet: http://twitter.com/jkrums/status/1121915133

Page 131:
"Zappos has been bought by Amazon for $928.000.000"
http://techcrunch.com/2009/07/22/amazon-buys-zappos/

Page 135:
Amazon's Kindle scandal
http://www.nytimes.com/2009/07/18/technology/
companies/18amazon.html

Page 151:
World of Warcraft: http://de.wikipedia.org/wiki/World_Of_Warcraft
Farmville: http://en.wikipedia.org/wiki/FarmVille

Pay what you want result:
http://blogs.bnet.com/intercom/?p=1214

Imprint

www.innovativethunder.com
twitter.com/innothunder
team@knarre.com

www.OhMyGodWhatHappened.com

www.PaywithaTweet.com

Print and Publishing:
Books on Demand GmbH, Norderstedt

ISBN: 9 7838 3918 4752

Die Deutsche Nationalbibliothek verzeichnet diese
Publikation in der Deutschen Nationalbibliografie;
detaillierte bibliografische Daten sind im Internet
über dnb.d-nb.de abrufbar.

THANKS.